Sports Illustrated KID$

SOCCER'S GREATEST

LAST-SECOND SHOTS

AND OTHER CRUNCH-TIME HEROICS

BY MATT CHANDLER

CAPSTONE PRESS
a capstone imprint

Captivate is published by Capstone Press, an imprint of Capstone.
1710 Roe Crest Drive, North Mankato, Minnesota 56003
www.capstonepub.com

Library of Congress Cataloging-in-Publication Data is available on the Library of Congress website.
ISBN 978-1-4966-8733-3 (hardcover)
ISBN 978-1-4966-8742-5 (paperback)
ISBN 978-1-4966-8743-2 (ebook PDF)

Summary: When victory is within reach and the game is in its final seconds, some players seize the moment and make themselves legends. From stunning goals in extra time to breathtaking saves in shootouts, some of soccer's greatest moments are chronicled in vivid fashion here. You've got a front-row view of the action.

Photo Credits
AP Photo: 25, Mark Lennihan, 39; Getty Images: AMA/Matthew Ashton, 37, FIFA/Alex Livesey, 7, FIFA/Steve Bardens, 29, Manchester City FC, 17, Offside/Mark Leech, 41, Tommy Cheng, 15; iStockphoto: isitsharp, cover (player); Newscom: Action Plus, 23, Actionplus/Tim Williams, 33, Kyodo, 26, USA Today Sports/Orlando Jorge Ramirez, 9, ZUMA Press/Fototricarico, 43, ZUMA Press/Lee Smith, 19; Shutterstock: Oleksandr Molotkovych, 44–45, silvae, cover (lights), 1, Vitaly Krivosheev, cover (stadium), 1; Sports Illustrated: Bob Martin, 21, Peter Read Miller, 5, 11, Robert Beck, 13, Simon Bruty, 31, 35

Editorial Credits
Bobbie Nuytten, designer; Eric Gohl, media researcher; Katy LaVigne, production specialist

All internet sites appearing in back matter were available and accurate when this book was sent to press.

Printed and bound in the USA.
PA117

TABLE OF CONTENTS

Words in **bold** are in the glossary.

FANTASTIC FINISHES

Soccer is the most popular sport in the world. It takes speed, skill, and **stamina**. It takes fancy footwork. A perfectly delivered pass. A sharp header. A kick that beats the goaltender or a clutch save.

Soccer's biggest moments are often game-winning plays. Some game-winners are set up by a defensive play. Some by a pass. Some by great single-player efforts. But they all have a common element: a ball ending up in the goal. A lot of game-winners come on power kicks. Others are headed or tapped into an open net. The reactions to game-winners are lively. One side is always happy—the other sad. There is nothing like thousands of fans cheering—or silenced by—a game-winning goal.

So let's explore the greatest crunch-time plays in soccer history, from the World Cup to Olympic Games. Jump in to find out about some of soccer's most heroic moments!

Members of the 1999 U.S. women's team celebrate their victory in the World Cup Finals.

CHAPTER 1

U.S. WOMEN'S HEROICS

ABBY SAVES THE DAY

The U.S. women's national team trailed Brazil late in their 2011 World Cup match. The score was 2–1, and it looked like Brazil would advance. Then, in the 122nd minute of the match, the United States broke through.

The United States came up with a steal. They quickly advanced the ball to midfield. Carli Lloyd sent a pass over to teammate Megan Rapinoe. She advanced the ball. She spied Abby Wambach breaking toward the goal. Four defenders were in good position for Brazil. It would take a perfect pass to connect with Wambach.

Could Rapinoe thread the ball through the defense? She answered that question with a perfect boot. It sailed high and hard. The leaping Wambach timed her jump. She pulled off a perfect header and knocked in the game-tying goal!

The last-second shot meant the game would be decided by penalty kicks. The teams traded penalty kicks. Finally American Ali Krieger ended it with a hard shot to the left corner. The U.S. advanced!

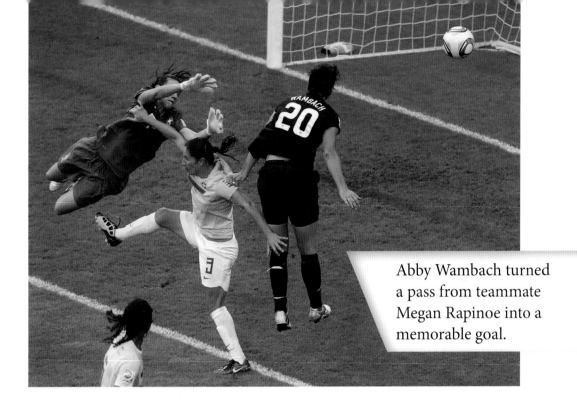

Abby Wambach turned a pass from teammate Megan Rapinoe into a memorable goal.

SHOOTOUT SCORES

When a soccer game is tied at the end of play, teams have a shootout. The rules are simple: Each team gets five kicks. Each kick must be taken by a different player. The team with the most goals wins the game. Shootouts are exciting for fans. It's a one-on-one battle of keeper versus kicker. No extra defense. No passing. Just one shot and one chance to stop it.

In 2013, Abby Wambach became the highest scorer in international soccer history—for women or men. Her record was broken by Canadian Christine Sinclair in 2020.

TOURNAMENT OF CHAMPIONS

The U.S. and Brazil national women's teams met in a 2017 Tournament of Nations match. Brazil led 2–0 with nine minutes left. Things looked rough for the U.S.

In the 79th minute of the match, American Christen Press scored. She hooked a shot inside the left bar for a big goal. The Americans still trailed by one. Press delivered again. This time she made a perfect pass. Press' teammate Megan Rapinoe knocked in the **equalizer** in the 84th minute!

The U.S. didn't stop there. Four minutes later, Rapinoe hit Kelley O'Hara with a pass in the corner. O'Hara put a shot on goal. The Brazilian goalie, Bárbara Micheline do Monte Barbosa, saved it. The rebound bounced right to American Julie Ertz. She drove the game-winner past Bárbara to give the U.S. an incredible win.

Julie Ertz first became a member of the U.S. women's national team in 2013. Through 2019, she had scored 19 goals in her national career.

Julie Ertz celebrates after scoring to lead the U.S. to victory over Brazil.

WOMEN ROCK (THE GOAL)

Seven star players in history have scored 100 goals as members of the women's national team. They are:

	PLAYER	GOALS	YEARS
1	Abby Wambach	184 goals	(2001–2015)
2	Mia Hamm	158 goals	(1987–2004)
3	Kristine Lilly	130 goals	(1987–2010)
4	Carli Lloyd	121 goals	(2005–present)
5	Michelle Akers	107 goals	(1985–2000)
6	Alex Morgan	107 goals	(2010–present)
7	Tiffeny Milbrett	100 goals	(1991–2005)

BRANDI BRINGS IT!

In 1999 the U.S. women's national team squared off against China. It was the World Cup Finals. The two teams battled for 90 minutes. At the end of the game, there was no score. The teams played through extra time. This was also scoreless. It was time for a shootout. Each team brought their five shooters to the field. More than 90,000 fans cheered wildly. It was the largest crowd to ever watch a women's sporting event in history.

The teams traded goals, each scoring on their first two penalty kicks. China's Liu Ying stepped to the ball. She drilled a hard kick. U.S. goaltender Briana Scurry dove and made the big save! The next three shooters scored for both teams. Brandi Chastain was the Americans' final shooter. The shootout was tied 4–4. If Chastain scored, the United States would win the World Cup.

Chastain prepared for the kick. China's goaltender, Gao Hong, stood in net. She had to stop Chastain's kick. If she failed, her team would lose the World Cup.

U.S. goalie Briana Scurry makes a save in the World Cup Finals.

As Chastain ran to the ball, Hong guessed she was kicking to the right corner and took a step toward that side. She was correct. But Chastain's kick was a rocket. Chastain connected and kept the ball low and hard. The ball traveled to the extreme corner. Even though Hong guessed correctly, the ball ripped passed her outstretched arms and into the net. The United States had won the World Cup!

Chastain pulled her shirt off and fell to her knees in celebration. It was an image that became a symbol of the American win. Many have called it the biggest goal in women's soccer history.

Growing up in California, Brandi Chastain played on the boys' soccer team in junior high. There was no girls' team.

PENALTY KICKS

Certain fouls that happen in the penalty area can lead to a penalty kick. Penalty kicks are dramatic moments. They are also **controversial**. There are no extra defenders, just a striker and a keeper. This creates the drama. The chances of scoring are very high. That creates the controversy. Opponents of penalty kicks say it's not fair to have games decided because of a single penalty.

Brandi Chastain after scoring in a shootout

AMERICA'S FIRST CUP

For many years, the United States was not highly respected in international soccer. In fact, no American team—men or women—won a world title or Olympic gold medal until 1991. That was the year the U.S. women's national team rose to the top.

It was the first year of the **FIFA** Women's World Cup. No one expected the U.S. to make it to the final. But the Americans beat every challenger. They earned shutouts of 7–0, 5–0, and 3–0. The U.S. met Norway for the final. More than 63,000 fans packed Tianhe Stadium in China for the match.

The United States played tough against Norway. Michelle Akers gave the Americans a 1–0 lead. Norway struck soon after to tie the game. Then, with two minutes left in regulation, the U.S. made history.

Akers took a long pass near Norway's goal. As she gathered the ball, she faced two defenders. Akers coolly beat them both. She then faked out goaltender Reidun Seth and walked in for an empty-net goal. This goal gave the underdog American women their first World Cup.

Carin Jennings (12) of the U.S. women's team tries to get past a sliding tackle by Anette Hansson of Sweden.

In 1991 the women's tournament wasn't originally called the World Cup. It was named the FIFA Women's World Championship for the M&Ms Cup.

CHAPTER 2
EUROPEAN MAGIC

PREMIER PERFORMANCE

In England, soccer rivalries are huge. Fans of the sport are loyal. The Premier League is England's highest level of soccer competition.

Manchester City was on the verge of winning the 2011–12 Premier League. They needed just one win. With a victory over Queens Park Rangers, the championship would be theirs! For much of the game, things looked bad for Man City. They trailed 2–1 late in the match. The title looked out of reach. Then they made a comeback.

After tying the game with a late goal, Man City had a chance at the championship. Attacking in QPR's end, Man City's Mario Balotelli slipped. As he fell to the ground, Balotelli passed. Teammate Sergio Agüero received the ball. With two defenders trailing him, Agüero delivered. He blazed a shot past the goaltender. The goal gave Manchester City the win and the Premier League title!

SHIRTS REQUIRED

Many soccer players slide across the pitch on their knees to celebrate a big goal. Others like to take off their shirts. Brandi Chastain famously did it in 1999 after winning the World Cup. Sergio Agüero went shirtless after scoring the Premiere League championship-winner for Manchester City in 2012. Since then, the removal of a jersey after scoring has been banned by FIFA. Any player who removes a jersey to celebrate receives a **yellow card**.

Sergio Agüero gets past a defender on his way to scoring a winning goal.

BIG BEN

Recovering from a broken leg, Wigan Athletic midfielder Ben Watson missed most of the 2012–13 Premier League season. He returned in time to help his team compete for the FA Cup. Standing in the way were defending champs Manchester City.

Wigan Athletic plays in the Championship League. This is a level below Man City's Premier League. But Wigan Athletic was there to compete. More than 86,000 fans went to the final. They packed Wembley Stadium in London. Wigan Athletic played Man City to a scoreless tie deep into the match. Late in the game, Watson came up huge.

Wigan Athletic midfielder Shaun Maloney prepared for a corner kick. He hit a solid ball, hooking it in front of Man City's net. Watson broke toward the goal. He timed his header perfectly and delivered a bullet. The ball rocketed past Man City's goaltender, Joe Hart. Wigan Athletic's huge upset won the FA Cup!

Ben Watson (left) watches his header find the goal to defeat Man City.

Wigan Athletic's championship was its first and only trip to the FA Cup Finals. Manchester City has won six FA Cups. Man City has also been runner-up five times.

STAR POWER

David Beckham was one of the most famous soccer players England had ever seen. He took the Premier League by storm. He played in the Olympics. He played for teams in Spain, the U.S., and France. He was a dominant player. He was a fashion model. He married a pop star. Beckham was a superstar on and off the pitch.

He was also a master at delivering when his team needed him most. Beckham was clutch under pressure. One of the biggest game-winners of his career came in a 2001 World Cup qualifier match against Greece. England was trailing 2–1 late. They didn't need to win the game. A draw would still earn them a spot in the World Cup.

With time almost up, England got a long-shot chance. A penalty was called against Greece. Beckham was awarded a **free kick**. This was a huge moment in Beckham's career. His relationship with English soccer fans was mixed. He was often booed. His loyalty was questioned. Beckham had the chance to erase all of that with a single kick.

David Beckham was a star for Manchester United early in his career.

Beckham stood nearly 30 yards from the net with a wall of bodies in front of him. It would take a perfect kick to beat Greece's goaltender, Antonios Nikopolidis. Beckham crushed it. He bent the kick left. Nikopolidis never had a chance. Beckham raced around the field celebrating his game-winning goal. England advanced to the World Cup.

Beckham scored 65 career goals on free kicks. The goal against Greece was one of seven career free-kick goals he scored for England's national team.

Beckham launches his legendary free kick against Greece.

KLAUS TO THE RESCUE

An equalizer is a goal that ties the score. Some of the best game-winning kicks would never have happen without an equalizer. With a history of nearly 100 years, the World Cup has seen plenty of amazing equalizers.

One of the biggest came in the 1982 semifinal match between West Germany and France. The West Germans trailed France 3–2. The match was in extra time. The West Germans needed a goal to keep their World Cup dreams alive.

With time running out, the West Germans advanced. Winger Pierre Littbarski delivered a kick to the box. Teammate Bernd Förster tried to head the ball into the net. Instead, it popped up in the air. Klaus Fischer was in the perfect spot. Fischer leaped high in the air. He delivered a perfect **bicycle kick**. The ball settled into the top corner of the net. West Germany had tied the game at three! Thanks to Fischer's big goal, West Germany won in penalty kicks. They advanced to the World Cup Final.

Klaus Fischer used a bicycle kick to score the tying goal in a 1982 World Cup semifinal match.

CHAPTER 3

OLYMPIC GOLD

HOMETOWN HERO

Brazil served as the host country for the 2016 Summer Olympics. The Brazil men's soccer team hoped to win gold as the "home" team. Brazilian soccer fans are passionate. They love their team when it wins. They get very upset when it loses.

Brazil's superstar forward in 2016 was Neymar da Silva Santos Júnior, known simply as Neymar. He was awesome in the 2016 Olympics. He scored four goals as Brazil advanced to the gold-medal match. There, Brazil took on Germany.

Neymar takes a free kick as Brazil faces Germany in the 2016 Olympic finals.

The final was to be decided by a shootout after neither side could break a 1–1 tie. Each team scored on their first four shootout attempts. Nils Petersen stepped up for Germany's fifth kick. He drilled a hard, low kick toward the right side of the net. Brazil's goaltender, Uilson Pedruzzi de Oliveira, dove. He knocked the ball away!

Neymar stepped up with the chance to bring his team the gold medal at home. The crowd of 63,000 fans went wild cheering. Neymar picked up the ball and gave it a kiss. Then he drove the winning kick into the top-right corner of the net. Brazil won the 2016 Olympic gold medal!

BRAZILIAN RESILIENCE

Two years before, in the 2014 World Cup, Brazil had to deal with epic failure. With Neymar leading the way, Brazil stormed to the semifinals. But after Neymar was injured with a broken back, Brazil was embarrassed, 7–1, by Germany. Things got so bad that Brazilian players were booed off the field by their own fans. Brazil's defeat of Germany at the 2016 Olympics, then, was all the sweeter.

SWEDISH DELIGHT

The U.S. women's national team was the favorite to win gold at the 2016 Olympics. Then they ran into a tough Swedish team in the quarterfinals. The road to gold hit a bump.

Regulation was a battle. At the end, the U.S. and Sweden were tied 1–1. The teams advanced to the shootout. It was a **knockout stage** match. The loser would not medal. It was an unusual spot for the Americans to be in. They medaled in every Olympiad since soccer was added as a women's sport in 1996. Also, the American women had won gold three times in a row. But now they were in danger. Losing would mean returning home without a medal. No gold. No silver. No bronze.

With the shootout tied 3–3, Sweden's Lisa Dahlkvist had a golden opportunity. As she approached the ball, U.S. goalkeeper Hope Solo broke to her right. Dahlkvist delivered a kick to the empty side of the net. It was the game-winner. The U.S. was stunned.

Lisa Dahlkvist of Sweden takes a penalty shot against the U.S.

Sweden also won the semifinals in penalty kicks. This time Brazil was the unfortunate loser. In the gold-medal game, Sweden's luck ran out. Germany won the gold, 2–1, leaving Sweden with silver.

MORGAN'S MAGIC

In 2012 Alex Morgan became a young star for the U.S. women's national team. In an early-year match versus a strong Canada squad, Morgan had a breakout performance. She scored two goals. She assisted on two more. The U.S. defeated Canada, 4–0. Morgan continued her strong play leading up to the Olympics. She recorded her first career **hat trick** in a match against Sweden.

The 2012 Olympics were held in London. The biggest soccer games of the year would happen there. On a U.S. team filled with veterans, the young Morgan stood out. She had just turned 23 years old in July, the same month the Olympic soccer competition began.

Alex Morgan

In the semifinal, the U.S. and Canada met again. The two North American clubs were tied 3–3 in extra time. Both were hoping to avoid a shootout. However, a shootout seemed likely. Time had nearly run out. With 38 seconds to go, a U.S. player chased the ball toward the corner. She gathered it and delivered a cross. Alex Morgan was sandwiched between two Canadian players. She leapt high in the air to meet the cross. The ball found the back of the net. Morgan had delivered a perfect header!

No one had ever scored a winning goal so late in a women's Olympic match. Thanks to Morgan's heroics, the Americans would be playing for gold! In the final, the U.S. played Japan. Carli Lloyd scored twice for the Americans. The U.S. captured gold with a 2–1 victory.

Alex Morgan was born on July 2, 1989, in San Dimas, California. She was the second-youngest player on the 2012 women's Olympic team. Sydney Leroux was the youngest.

Morgan (second from left) scores on a header against Canada.

DONOVAN DELIVERS

The final minutes in a 2010 FIFA World Cup match ticked away. The United States and Algeria were locked in a scoreless battle. Algeria advanced the ball deep. One of Algeria's forwards got behind the U.S. defense. He found himself wide open and took a shot at a game-winner.

Smack! The kick hit the crossbar! The Americans were still alive.

A moment later U.S. striker Clint Dempsey had a chance to be the hero. At the other end of the pitch, Dempsey got free. He buried a shot in the back of the net. Game over! But wait . . . the officials ruled Dempsey offside. The goal was waved off.

Play resumed. Algeria attacked again. A header was stopped by the U.S. keeper. The keeper threw an overhead pass and the Americans were off and running. U.S. forward Landon Donovan took the ball past midfield. He passed ahead, and the ball went to Dempsey. Dempsey took a low shot. It bounded off the Algerian keeper and went straight to Donovan. Donovan calmly directed it into the empty side of the net. The Americans had pulled off a thrilling 1–0 win!

Landon Donovan closes in on the ball moments before scoring against Algeria in the World Cup.

RIDING THE BICYCLE

The Panama men's team played a match against the United States in the 2019 Gold Cup tournament. Panama was the underdog. The U.S. had beaten the team from Panama easily in their last two matchups. But this time Panama battled. With 65 minutes played, there was no score.

American Djordje Mihailovic lifted a corner kick into the air. The ball was headed toward the goal. Panama's goaltender, José Calderón, had a chance to collect the loose ball. Calderón missed it. American Jozy Altidore was there. But he was facing away from the goal. No problem. He leaped in the air. He scissor-kicked a shot backward, over his head.

The bicycle kick rocketed toward the goal. Calderón never had a chance. Goal! Panama never scored, and the U.S. advanced. The 17,000 fans in Kansas City were treated to one of the most exciting goals possible.

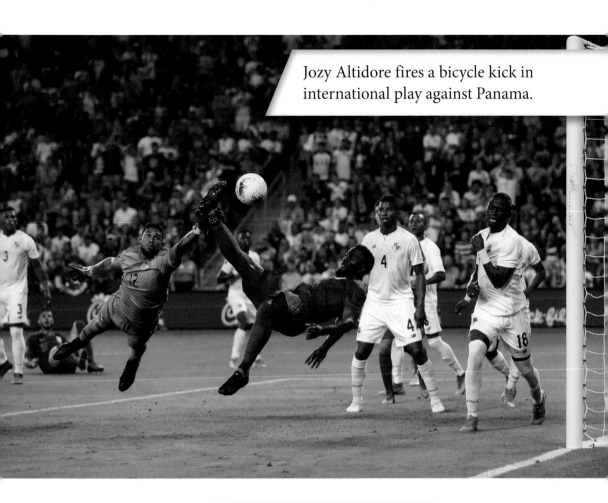

Jozy Altidore fires a bicycle kick in international play against Panama.

ORIGINS OF THE BICYCLE KICK

The bicycle kick dates back more than a hundred years. Some say Ramón Unzaga of Chile was the first player to kick the ball backward over his head, in 1914. There are other claims that a player from Callao, Peru, invented it before 1900. The move was said to have come in a game played against British sailors.

BREAKING THE DROUGHT

The U.S. men's national team hadn't qualified for the World Cup since 1950. But the 1990 team was just one win away from earning a spot in the World Cup. All it would take was a victory in a qualifier match. The opponent? Trinidad.

The two teams engaged. The first 25 minutes were scoreless. For the United States, a tie would be the same as a loss. They had to win to qualify. Just before halftime, U.S. defender Paul Caligiuri took a pass from teammate Tab Ramos. A Trinidad defender was on him.

Caligiuri made some magic. He faked out his opponent by switching the ball from his right foot to his left. Once past the crossed-up defender, he took a left-footed shot on the goal. It curved down and into the top of the goal. The U.S. had a 1–0 lead!

The U.S. held on to win. Caligiuri's shot was nicknamed "The Shot Heard 'round the World." It is one of the most famous goals in U.S. soccer history.

WORLD CUP WARRIORS

Beginning in 1990, the U.S. men's team appeared in seven consecutive World Cup tournaments. (The 2018 team did not qualify for the tournament.) Here is a look at where they finished in each tournament in the field of 32 teams after 1990:

YEAR	WON	LOST	TIED	PLACE
1990	0	3	0	23rd
1994	1	2	1	14th
1998	0	3	0	32nd
2002	2	2	1	8th
2006	0	2	1	25th
2010	1	1	2	12th
2014	1	2	1	15th

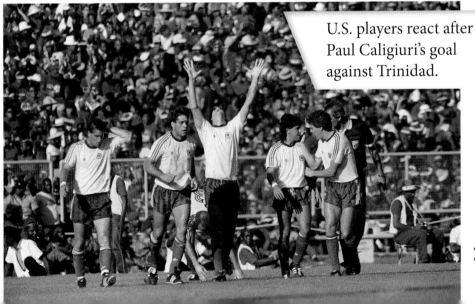

U.S. players react after Paul Caligiuri's goal against Trinidad.

CHAPTER 5

THE BEST OF THE REST

POWER UNDER PRESSURE

Sometimes in soccer, simply winning isn't enough. Championships can be decided by who scored more goals. In 1989 that was the case for Arsenal. The British club needed to win by two goals over Liverpool to claim the 1989 Premier League title. Late in the match, Arsenal led 1–0. If they couldn't score again, they would win the match but lose the championship.

Arsenal made one last rush. Lee Dixon delivered a long pass. Alan Smith fielded it. Smith was the club's leading scorer. But he chose to pass. He found midfielder Michael Thomas.

With time running out, Thomas nabbed the high pass with his foot. A Liverpool defender threatened. Thomas raced past. Before Liverpool could recover, he blasted the game-winner home! Arsenal won 2–0. The Premier League title was theirs.

Arsenal's Michael Thomas carries a young fan after clinching the Premier League championship.

Arsenal was formed in 1886. A unit of cannon makers organized the team.

CLUTCH KICK

Many consider Cristiano Ronaldo the best men's soccer player of our time. He began playing for Portugal's national team in 2003. In 2019 Ronaldo scored his 700th career goal. He is one of only six men in the history of the game to do that.

One of Ronaldo's 700 club goals was a game-winner in 2019. It helped his club, Juventus, earn a big win. With under a minute left in the match, Ronaldo made his move. He tapped in what looked like the game-winning goal. But the superstar was offside. The goal was waved off.

Amazingly, Ronaldo found another chance. He worked his way into position for one last shot. But then he was tripped. That set up a last-second penalty kick. With the game on the line, Ronaldo delivered. His penalty kick just snuck by the diving Genoa goaltender. Juventus escaped with a 2–1 win.

Cristiano Ronaldo in action

GOAL-SCORING KINGS

Will Cristiano Ronaldo end his career as the men's all-time international goal-scorer? Many fans think so. Here is a look at the top five leaders in international goals in men's soccer, all-time.

	PLAYER	GOALS	COUNTRY
1	Ali Daei	109	Iran
2	Cristiano Ronaldo	99	Portugal
3	Ferenc Puskás	84	Hungary and Spain
4	Kunishige Kamamoto	80	Japan
5	Godfrey Chitalu	79	Zambia

GOALS AROUND THE WORLD

Soccer is truly a global game. Players from 16 countries come together to compete at the Olympics. There are also international competitions between countries. This map shows every country that has won an Olympic gold medal in soccer.

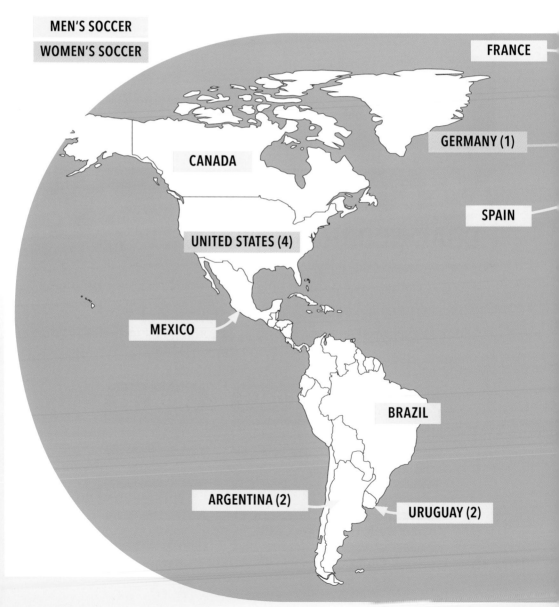

MEN'S SOCCER

WOMEN'S SOCCER

FRANCE

GERMANY (1)

CANADA

SPAIN

UNITED STATES (4)

MEXICO

BRAZIL

ARGENTINA (2)

URUGUAY (2)

GREAT BRITAIN (3)

NORWAY (1)

SWEDEN

BELGIUM

POLAND

RUSSIA/SOVIET UNION (2)

CZECHOSLOVAKIA*

HUNGARY (3)

EAST GERMANY**

ITALY

YUGOSLAVIA***

NIGERIA

CAMEROON

*Czechoslovakia split into two countries (Czech Republic and Slovak Republic) in 1993.

**East Germany and West Germany united in 1990.

***In the early 1990s, Yugoslavia broke apart into several independent countries.

GLOSSARY

bicycle kick (BY-sy-kel KIK)—a kick in which the player somersaults backward and moves his or her legs in a pedaling motion to kick the ball in midair

controversial (kon-truh-VUR-shuhl)—causing dispute or disagreement

equalizer (EE-kwul-eyes-er)—a score that ties a game

extra time (EK-struh TYME)—the overtime period played if the score remains tied after 90 minutes of play

free kick (FREE KICK)—a way of restarting play; a free kick is awarded after a violation of rules by the opposing team

FIFA (FEE-FAH)—international group that governs soccer; it stands for Fédération Internationale de Football Association

hat trick (HAT TRIK)—when a player scores three goals in one game

knockout stage (NOK-out STAYJ)—after group play in a World Cup tournament, top teams advance to the second stage, in which a single loss eliminates teams from the competition

stamina (STAM-uh-nuh)—the energy and strength to keep doing something for a long time

yellow card (YEL-oh KARD)—an official warning that a player has broken the rules; the referee holds up a yellow piece of yellow plastic or cardboard to show that a warning has been given

READ MORE

Chandler, Matt. *Alex Morgan: Soccer Champion*. North Mankato, MN: Capstone Press, 2020.

Mikoley, Kate. *Soccer: Stats, Facts, and Figures*. New York: Gareth Stevens Publishing, 2018.

Williams, Heather. *Soccer: A Guide for Players and Fans*. North Mankato, MN: Capstone Press, 2020.

INTERNET SITES

European Leagues
www.europeanleagues.com

Major League Soccer
www.mlssoccer.com

National Women's Soccer League
www.nwslsoccer.com

INDEX